Spot the Shape

Shapes in Art

Rebecca Rissman

www.raintreepublishers.co.uk

Visit our website to find out
more information about
Raintree books.

To order:

☎ Phone 0845 6044371
🖷 Fax +44 (0) 1865 312263
🖳 Email myorders@capstonepub.co.uk

Customers from outside the UK please telephone +44 1865 312262

Edited by Rebecca Rissman, Charlotte Guillain and Catherine Veitch
Designed by Joanna Hinton-Malivoire
Picture research by Tracy Cummins and Heather Mauldin
Originated by Dot Gradations Ltd
Printed in China by South China Printing Company Ltd

ISBN 978 0 43119288 8 (hardback)
13 12 11 10 09
10 9 8 7 6 5 4 3 2 1

ISBN 978 0 431 19294 9 (paperback)
14 13 12 11 10
10 9 8 7 6 5 4 3 2 1

British Library Cataloguing in Publication Data
Rissman, Rebecca
Shapes in art. - (Acorn. Spot the shape)
516.1'5
A full catalogue record for this book is available from the British Library.

Acknowledgements
We would like to thank the following for permission to reproduce photographs: ©Alamy pp. **4** (Freefall Images), **15** (1), **16** (1), **23b** (1); ©Bettina Strenske pp. **17**, **18**; ©Heinemann Raintree p. **21** (David Rigg); ©Jupiter p. **6** (Robert Harding Images/Jane Sweeney); ©Jupiter Images pp. **11** (Corbis), **12** (Corbis); ©Shutterstock pp. **9** (Michael Rubin), **10** (Michael Rubin), **13** (Zeber), **14** (Zeber), **19** (Franck Boston), **20** (Franck Boston); ©The Bridgeman Art Library International pp. **7** (The Trustees of the Goodwood Collection), **8** (The Trustees of the Goodwood Collection), **23a** (The Trustees of the Goodwood Collection).

Cover photograph of Factories, 1926 (oil on card) reproduced with permission of ©The Bridgeman Art Library International/Seiwert, Franz W. (1894-1933)/Hamburger Kunsthalle, Hamburg, Germany. Back cover photograph of diamond pattern cloth reproduced with permission of ©Jupiter Images/Corbis.

Every effort has been made to contact copyright holders of material reproduced in this book. Any omissions will be rectified in subsequent printings if notice is given to the publishers.

Contents

Shapes

There are shapes all around us.

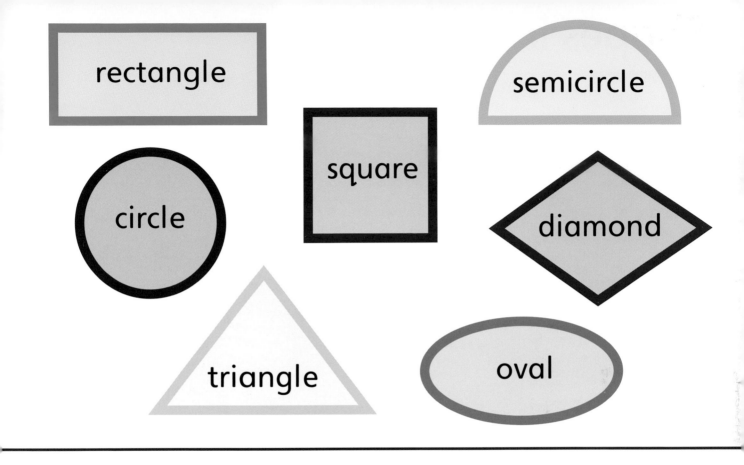

rectangle

semicircle

circle

square

diamond

triangle

oval

Each shape has a name.

Shapes in art

There are many shapes in art.

What shape is this picture frame?

This picture frame is an oval.

What shape is the cherry on
this sculpture?

The cherry on this sculpture is
a circle.

What shapes are in this cloth?

There are diamonds in this cloth.

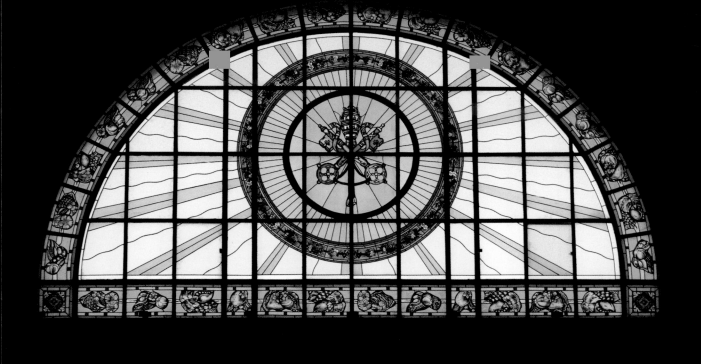

What shape is this window?

This window is a semicircle.

What shape is in this sculpture?

A rectangle is in this sculpture.

What shapes is this man painting?

This man is painting triangles.

What shapes are in this sculpture?

There are squares in this sculpture.

There are many shapes in art.

What shapes can you see?

Naming shapes

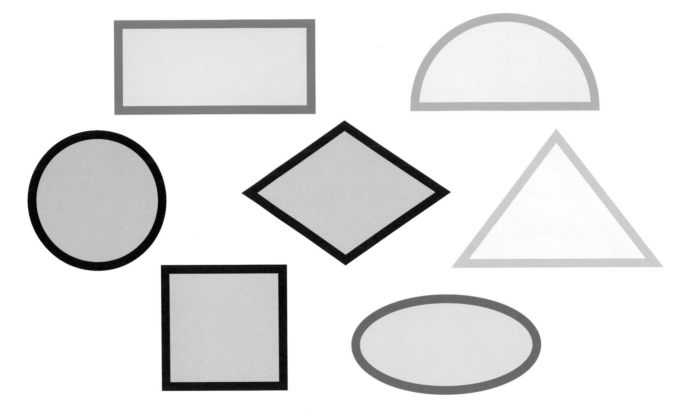

Can you remember the names of these shapes?

Picture glossary

frame piece of wood or metal around the edge of a picture

sculpture model that an artist carves or makes out of material like stone, wood, or clay

Index

G- I. F.

Notes for parents and teachers

Before reading

Make a set of the shapes shown on page 22 out of card. Hold up each shape in turn to the class and ask the children what it is called. Pass each shape round for the children to handle. Teach the children this poem and hold up the relevant shape as you sing: "Do you know what shape this is, what shape this is, what shape this is? Do you know what shape this is. I'm holding in my hand? Yes I know what shape it is, what shape it is, what shape it is. Yes, I know what shape it is. You're holding up a…"

After reading

• Show the children how to make a shape person. Cut different shapes from coloured card, and encourage the children to choose different shapes for parts of the body.

• Look through art books and posters and ask the children to look for shapes. For example, show the children the painting *Soft Hard* by Wassily Kandinsky.

• Take the children on a shape search round the school or on the way to school. Give each child one card shape and ask him or her to find a matching shape. Make a class list of all the shapes they find.